D1612261

FOUR PROGRESS

WORRY IV NOTHING
own your thoughts

this journal belongs to:

_____

Published by Four Progress, LLC
ISBN 978-1-7923-3949-3
First Edition
Designed in New England
Printed in China

www.fourprogress.com
email us at hello@fourprogress.com

Thoughts:

They don't ask for permission or give advance notice.
They don't care who or where we are.
They often weigh us down.

Some thoughts can be positive and productive - but many aren't. All too often, the bad ones pop into our heads without warning. These unexpected, intrusive, often negative thoughts that latch onto our brains and don't let go - they have a name:

Automatic thoughts.

We call them automatic because, without consciously creating them, they appear and take up valuable space inside our minds. We've all had automatic thoughts before. Sometimes at the worst possible moments:

Before a big presentation.   *I'm not good at my job.*
In the middle of an important dinner.   *I'm never going to be skinny.*
Laying in bed, trying desperately to fall asleep.   *I feel so alone.*

All of these are examples of negative automatic thoughts. Many of us have them every day. But, regardless of how real these automatic thoughts can feel, or how true they might seem, they're often *inaccurate*.

Completely stopping these automatic thoughts from entering our minds might be difficult, but there is a way for us to change the way we process them.

The **Worry IV Nothing**© journal by **Four Progress, LLC**™ was designed to do just that.

Worry IV Nothing© uses powerful cognitive restructuring tactics at the heart of cognitive behavioral therapy (CBT). CBT aims to change unhelpful intrapersonal distortions, improve emotional regulation and develop coping strategies to solve difficult problems. The pages ahead will help us document and deconstruct our automatic thoughts - then teach us to interpret and rebuild them in a more balanced, accurate way.

While this journal can be used independently, we recommend using it in collaboration with a licensed mental health professional.

Worry IV Nothing© is a way of taking back control of our thoughts, a way of improving our mindfulness and well-being, and a way of making a little bit of *fourward* progress - with every turn of the page.

How to use this journal

The goal of this journal is to teach us how to break free of negative thinking patterns resulting from automatic thoughts. Each spread of pages features prompts to take us through the four steps of cognitive restructuring:

I. Articulation
Helping us get our thoughts organized and down on paper.

Date, day, time and location
Here, time and location stamping sets important context for our entry. It makes it easy to look back at prior pages, and quickly make connections between correlating automatic thought patterns. Date, time, location - a simple but critical first step.

So, what's going on?
Set the stage here. Did something unexpected happen during the day? Did someone send us a cryptic message we still don't quite understand? Summarize events, actions and people involved to understand what triggered us to have the negative automatic thought in the first place.

II. Awareness
Helping us slow down and become aware of our physical and emotional feelings.

Ok. Describe how you're feeling.
It helps to ground ourselves first in the physical sensations we experience (i.e. rapid heart rate) and then focus on emotions (i.e. anxiousness). Connecting the body and mind in this way is foundational to cognitive behavioral therapy.

Now, what are you thinking?
This is where we introduce our automatic thought. The thought might be verbal self talk, an image in our mind or even a troubling memory. For example, if a friend didn't respond to our last text message our automatic thought might be: *oh no, I said something wrong. Elizabeth must be mad at me.* Try to jot down every single detail.

III. Analysis
Helping us gain a sense of control by reflecting rather than reacting.

What evidence supports that thought?
Here's where we give our brain some credit. We don't censor ourselves. Why might these automatic thoughts be true? Some reasons may seem better than others, but write all of them down. Keep asking yourself what evidence exists that makes us believe this thought.

What about evidence that contradicts it?
Now take the other side. Make a list of reasons why this thought may not be 100% true. It might be helpful to ask: *if a friend thought this about themself, what would I say to him or her? Have there been times when this thought wasn't true in the past?*

IV. Adjustment
Helping us break the negative chain reaction by substituting accurate thoughts.

Got it. Let's try writing down an alternative thought:
Examine the side-by-side lists. Does our initial automatic thought seem valid? Ask: *given all the evidence, is there a better way of evaluating this situation?* Transcribing the details in this way will allow us to practice mental flexibility, a critical step to changing our negative thought patterns.

Remember, it's not about thinking happy thoughts. It's about thinking more *accurate* thoughts, and understanding how and why our thoughts have become biased in some way. Using the text message example, this could become: *maybe Elizabeth is busy or didn't see my text. If she were mad at me she would tell me* - or even *she might have misunderstood my text, but I know that I did my best to express myself.*

How do you feel now?
After we've generated an alternative thought, it helps to go back and look at our original feelings, the physical and emotional ones from Step II. Our uneasy feelings might not totally vanish but, in most cases, they at least subside in intensity. Write down any changes felt during the exercise, taking note of signs of relief from the negativity as a way of reinforcing our new restructuring habit.

Anything else before you go?

When we close this journal we signal to our brains that this thought is done - that there is no more ruminating or negative feelings to be had. We've generated a more realistic thought and we can move on. But, before we do that completely, we find it can be helpful to have a little space for ourselves. Sometimes we write something we are grateful for, sometimes it's something to keep in mind for next time - and sometimes we give ourselves the space to acknowledge the changes we are making, for progress.

Disclaimer

This journal is filled with blank pages. A blank page is a powerful thing, if used correctly.

Although the techniques used in this journal are for any of us looking to improve our thinking habits, its pages are not a replacement for a therapist. In fact, in many cases, it serves as a collaboration tool to be used alongside a licensed therapist. Always seek out the advice of your own mental health provider if you have any questions or concerns about a medical condition or mental disorder. Never disregard professional medical advice or delay seeking it in lieu of this journal.

Useful journaling tips

Before you jump into the following pages, we want to leave you with a few tips that we've found helpful using the journal ourselves.

I. Practice, practice, practice

Just like most learned skills, cognitive restructuring requires practice. Remember: the ultimate goal is to fundamentally change the way we think. To own our thoughts. This won't happen overnight, and we need to continue to come back to these pages until developing alternate thoughts becomes habit.

II. Believable alternative thoughts

Another important reminder: this is not a positive thinking exercise. It's an exercise in realistic thinking. When it comes to alternative thoughts, it's critical they are believable. It may be challenging at times, but being honest with our thoughts is the goal. An example: *this may not work out in my favor, but I have the strength and fortitude to get through it.*

III. One thought at a time

Don't spend too much time over-analyzing each thought. And, don't try to squish multiple automatic thoughts into one exercise. Focus on *one* thought and spend 5-10 minutes going through the exercises. If we spend too much time ruminating over every detail, this process will feel laborious and we become less likely to form this new habit.

IV. Progress over perfection

It's common to have high expectations, and to compare ourselves with others. But, when we do that, we often lose sight of our own value and accomplishments. When you use this journal, try to focus on progress across multiple entries, not just what lives on a single page. Remind yourself: *progress isn't linear.* There will be good days when we own our thoughts, and bad days when our thoughts feel out of control. But with every page we turn, and every thought we tackle, we become better versions of ourselves. We do it for progress.

date June 1, 2020   day (circle one)   sun   (mon)   tue   wed   thu   fri   sat

time 10:15 pm   where are you right now? Sitting on my couch

so, what's going on? I just got back from my friend, Sarah's, house. She invited a small group of her friends over for drinks and board games. When I arrived I realized that I was the only one there without a significant other. It was so awkward when we needed to pair off into teams because I was the odd man out. I decided to just watch the game instead of play because I didn't want to be any one's third wheel. Even some of her friends that are way younger than me are in serious long-term relationships.

ok. describe how you're feeling: My heart is racing and feels heavy. I feel like I am on the verge of tears. Of all the emotions I am feeling, I most strongly feel anxious and worried. I also feel discouraged, ashamed, embarrassed and lonely.

now, what are you thinking? Something is wrong with me. I am a loser, a loner. No one will ever love me and I will end up alone.

IV

what evidence supports that thought?

· Everyone at the party tonight had a significant other besides me
· I haven't had a boyfriend in a while
· The last time I liked a guy he didn't like me back
· My family members always pressure me about my dating life, like they are worried about my single-ness
· I don't really like going to bars and meeting new people

what about evidence that contradicts it?

· I have a lot of friends that enjoy spending time with me
· Last time I went out a guy asked for my number
· I was the one that broke off my last relationship because it didn't feel right
· My aunt didn't meet her husband until she was much older than me
· Not all my friends are in serious relationships, I'm not the only single one

got it. let's try writing down an alternative thought: I haven't really been trying to meet anyone new. I can put more effort into meeting someone, but even if I don't right away, that doesn't mean I will end up alone... forever. It just may take me a bit more time and that is okay.

how do you feel now? I feel a little less anxious. I realize now that I am in control of my time. If I want to be in a relationship, I can go out and put in more effort. I also realize that I am not the only single person I know. I just happened to be in a situation that made me feel like that was the case.

anything else before you go? I am grateful that I have time for myself. Being single means I get to choose whatever I want to watch on tv, eat whatever I want for dinner and spend my time freely. Next time I am in this situation I will try to remember that it is okay to be single and it does not mean something is wrong with me.

IV

date _____   day (circle one)   sun   mon   tue   wed   thu   fri   sat

time _____   where are you right now? _____

so, what's going on? _____
_____
_____
_____
_____
_____
_____
_____
_____
_____
_____

ok. describe how you're feeling: _____
_____
_____
_____
_____
_____
_____
_____

now, what are you thinking? _____
_____
_____
_____
_____
_____

what evidence supports that thought?

_____
_____
_____
_____
_____
_____
_____
_____
_____
_____
_____
_____

what about evidence that contradicts it?

_____
_____
_____
_____
_____
_____
_____
_____
_____
_____
_____
_____

got it. let's try writing down an alternative thought: _____

_____
_____
_____
_____
_____

how do you feel now? _____

_____
_____

anything else before you go? _____

_____
_____
_____

date _____ day (circle one)   sun   mon   tue   wed   thu   fri   sat

time _____ where are you right now? _____

so, what's going on? _____

_____

_____

_____

_____

_____

_____

_____

_____

_____

ok. describe how you're feeling: _____

_____

_____

_____

_____

_____

_____

_____

now, what are you thinking? _____

_____

_____

_____

_____

what evidence supports that thought?

_____
_____
_____
_____
_____
_____
_____
_____
_____
_____
_____

what about evidence that contradicts it?

_____
_____
_____
_____
_____
_____
_____
_____
_____
_____
_____

got it. let's try writing down an alternative thought: _____

_____
_____
_____
_____
_____

how do you feel now? _____

_____
_____

anything else before you go? _____

_____
_____
_____
_____

date _____ day (circle one)   sun   mon   tue   wed   thu   fri   sat

time _____ where are you right now? _____

so, what's going on? _____

_____

_____

_____

_____

_____

_____

_____

_____

_____

ok. describe how you're feeling: _____

_____

_____

_____

_____

_____

_____

_____

now, what are you thinking? _____

_____

_____

_____

_____

what evidence supports that thought?

_____

_____

_____

_____

_____

_____

_____

_____

_____

_____

_____

what about evidence that contradicts it?

_____

_____

_____

_____

_____

_____

_____

_____

_____

_____

_____

got it. let's try writing down an alternative thought: _____

_____

_____

_____

_____

_____

how do you feel now? _____

_____

_____

anything else before you go? _____

_____

_____

_____

date _____   day (circle one)   sun   mon   tue   wed   thu   fri   sat

time _____   where are you right now? _____

so, what's going on? _____

_____

_____

_____

_____

_____

_____

_____

_____

_____

ok. describe how you're feeling: _____

_____

_____

_____

_____

_____

_____

_____

now, what are you thinking? _____

_____

_____

_____

_____

what evidence supports that thought?   what about evidence that contradicts it?

_____   _____
_____   _____
_____   _____
_____   _____
_____   _____
_____   _____
_____   _____
_____   _____
_____   _____
_____   _____
_____   _____

got it. let's try writing down an alternative thought: _____

_____
_____
_____
_____
_____

how do you feel now? _____

_____
_____
_____

anything else before you go? _____

_____
_____
_____
_____

IV

date _____   day (circle one)   sun   mon   tue   wed   thu   fri   sat

time _____   where are you right now? _____

so, what's going on? _____
_____
_____
_____
_____
_____
_____
_____
_____
_____
_____

ok. describe how you're feeling: _____
_____
_____
_____
_____
_____
_____
_____

now, what are you thinking? _____
_____
_____
_____
_____

what evidence supports that thought?

what about evidence that contradicts it?

_____

_____

_____

_____

_____

_____

_____

_____

_____

_____

_____

got it. let's try writing down an alternative thought: _____

_____

_____

_____

_____

_____

how do you feel now? _____

_____

_____

anything else before you go? _____

_____

_____

_____

date _____   day (circle one)   sun   mon   tue   wed   thu   fri   sat

time _____   where are you right now? _____

so, what's going on? _____
_____
_____
_____
_____
_____
_____
_____
_____
_____

ok. describe how you're feeling: _____
_____
_____
_____
_____
_____
_____
_____

now, what are you thinking? _____
_____
_____
_____
_____
_____

what evidence supports that thought?

what about evidence that contradicts it?

_____
_____
_____
_____
_____
_____
_____
_____
_____
_____
_____

got it. let's try writing down an alternative thought: _____

_____
_____
_____
_____
_____
_____

how do you feel now? _____

_____
_____

anything else before you go? _____

_____
_____
_____

IV

date _____ day (circle one)   sun   mon   tue   wed   thu   fri   sat

time _____ where are you right now? _____

so, what's going on? _____
_____
_____
_____
_____
_____
_____
_____
_____
_____

ok. describe how you're feeling: _____
_____
_____
_____
_____
_____
_____
_____

now, what are you thinking? _____
_____
_____
_____
_____

what evidence supports that thought?

_____
_____
_____
_____
_____
_____
_____
_____
_____
_____

what about evidence that contradicts it?

_____
_____
_____
_____
_____
_____
_____
_____
_____
_____

got it. let's try writing down an alternative thought: _____

_____
_____
_____
_____
_____

how do you feel now? _____

_____
_____
_____

anything else before you go? _____

_____
_____
_____

date _____ day (circle one)   sun   mon   tue   wed   thu   fri   sat

time _____ where are you right now? _____

so, what's going on? _____

_____

_____

_____

_____

_____

_____

_____

_____

_____

ok. describe how you're feeling: _____

_____

_____

_____

_____

_____

_____

_____

now, what are you thinking? _____

_____

_____

_____

_____

what evidence supports that thought?

what about evidence that contradicts it?

_____

_____

_____

_____

_____

_____

_____

_____

_____

_____

_____

got it. let's try writing down an alternative thought: _____

_____

_____

_____

_____

_____

how do you feel now? _____

_____

_____

anything else before you go? _____

_____

_____

_____

date _____ day (circle one)   sun   mon   tue   wed   thu   fri   sa

time _____ where are you right now? _____

so, what's going on? _____
_____
_____
_____
_____
_____
_____
_____
_____
_____

ok. describe how you're feeling: _____
_____
_____
_____
_____
_____
_____
_____

now, what are you thinking? _____
_____
_____
_____
_____

what evidence supports that thought?

_____
_____
_____
_____
_____
_____
_____
_____
_____
_____
_____
_____

what about evidence that contradicts it?

_____
_____
_____
_____
_____
_____
_____
_____
_____
_____
_____
_____

got it. let's try writing down an alternative thought: _____

_____
_____
_____
_____
_____

how do you feel now? _____

_____
_____
_____

anything else before you go? _____

_____
_____
_____
_____

use this page to reflect on the progress you've made.
have you idenfitied recurring triggers and anxious feelings?
are you starting to think in a more constructive way?

tell me about it.

_____

_____

_____

_____

_____

_____

_____

_____

_____

_____

_____

_____

_____

_____

_____

_____

_____

_____

_____

_____

_____

_____

_____

_____

_____

_____

_____

_____

_____

date _____   day (circle one)   sun   mon   tue   wed   thu   fri   sat

time _____   where are you right now? _____

so, what's going on? _____

_____

_____

_____

_____

_____

_____

_____

_____

_____

ok. describe how you're feeling: _____

_____

_____

_____

_____

_____

_____

_____

now, what are you thinking? _____

_____

_____

_____

_____

what evidence supports that thought? what about evidence that contradicts it?

_____ _____
_____ _____
_____ _____
_____ _____
_____ _____
_____ _____
_____ _____
_____ _____
_____ _____
_____ _____
_____ _____

got it. let's try writing down an alternative thought: _____

_____
_____
_____
_____
_____

how do you feel now? _____

_____
_____
_____

anything else before you go? _____

_____
_____
_____
_____

date _____   day (circle one)   sun   mon   tue   wed   thu   fri   sat

time _____   where are you right now? _____

so, what's going on? _____

_____

_____

_____

_____

_____

_____

_____

_____

_____

_____

ok. describe how you're feeling: _____

_____

_____

_____

_____

_____

_____

_____

_____

now, what are you thinking? _____

_____

_____

_____

_____

what evidence supports that thought?   what about evidence that contradicts it?

_____   _____
_____   _____
_____   _____
_____   _____
_____   _____
_____   _____
_____   _____
_____   _____
_____   _____
_____   _____
_____   _____

got it. let's try writing down an alternative thought: _____

_____
_____
_____
_____
_____

how do you feel now? _____

_____
_____

anything else before you go? _____

_____
_____
_____

date _____ day (circle one)   sun   mon   tue   wed   thu   fri   sa

time _____ where are you right now? _____

so, what's going on? _____

_____

_____

_____

_____

_____

_____

_____

_____

_____

_____

ok. describe how you're feeling: _____

_____

_____

_____

_____

_____

_____

_____

_____

now, what are you thinking? _____

_____

_____

_____

_____

_____

what evidence supports that thought?

_____
_____
_____
_____
_____
_____
_____
_____
_____
_____
_____
_____
_____

what about evidence that contradicts it?

_____
_____
_____
_____
_____
_____
_____
_____
_____
_____
_____
_____
_____

got it. let's try writing down an alternative thought: _____

_____
_____
_____
_____
_____
_____

how do you feel now? _____

_____
_____
_____

anything else before you go? _____

_____
_____
_____
_____

date _____ day (circle one)　　sun　　mon　　tue　　wed　　thu　　fri　　sat

time _____ where are you right now? _____

so, what's going on? _____
_____
_____
_____
_____
_____
_____
_____
_____
_____

ok. describe how you're feeling: _____
_____
_____
_____
_____
_____
_____
_____

now, what are you thinking? _____
_____
_____
_____
_____

what evidence supports that thought?

what about evidence that contradicts it?

_____
_____
_____
_____
_____
_____
_____
_____
_____
_____
_____
_____

got it. let's try writing down an alternative thought: _____

_____
_____
_____
_____
_____

how do you feel now? _____

_____
_____

anything else before you go? _____

_____
_____
_____

ℕ

date _____ day (circle one) sun mon tue wed thu fri sat

time _____ where are you right now? _____

so, what's going on? _____

_____

_____

_____

_____

_____

_____

_____

_____

_____

ok. describe how you're feeling: _____

_____

_____

_____

_____

_____

_____

_____

now, what are you thinking? _____

_____

_____

_____

_____

_____

what evidence supports that thought?

what about evidence that contradicts it?

_____

_____

_____

_____

_____

_____

_____

_____

_____

_____

_____

_____

_____

_____

_____

_____

_____

_____

_____

_____

_____

_____

got it. let's try writing down an alternative thought: _____

_____

_____

_____

_____

_____

_____

how do you feel now? _____

_____

_____

_____

anything else before you go? _____

_____

_____

_____

_____

IV

date _____   day (circle one)   sun   mon   tue   wed   thu   fri   sa

time _____   where are you right now? _____

so, what's going on? _____

_____

_____

_____

_____

_____

_____

_____

_____

_____

ok. describe how you're feeling: _____

_____

_____

_____

_____

_____

_____

_____

now, what are you thinking? _____

_____

_____

_____

_____

what evidence supports that thought?

_____
_____
_____
_____
_____
_____
_____
_____
_____
_____
_____

what about evidence that contradicts it?

_____
_____
_____
_____
_____
_____
_____
_____
_____
_____
_____

got it. let's try writing down an alternative thought: _____

_____
_____
_____
_____
_____
_____

how do you feel now? _____

_____
_____
_____

anything else before you go? _____

_____
_____
_____
_____

date _____   day (circle one)   sun   mon   tue   wed   thu   fri   sat

time _____   where are you right now? _____

so, what's going on? _____

_____

_____

_____

_____

_____

_____

_____

_____

_____

ok. describe how you're feeling: _____

_____

_____

_____

_____

_____

_____

_____

now, what are you thinking? _____

_____

_____

_____

_____

_____

what evidence supports that thought?   what about evidence that contradicts it?

_____   _____
_____   _____
_____   _____
_____   _____
_____   _____
_____   _____
_____   _____
_____   _____
_____   _____
_____   _____
_____   _____

got it. let's try writing down an alternative thought: _____

_____
_____
_____
_____
_____
_____

how do you feel now? _____

_____
_____
_____

anything else before you go? _____

_____
_____
_____
_____

$\mathbb{IV}$

date _____   day (circle one)   sun   mon   tue   wed   thu   fri   sat

time _____   where are you right now? _____

so, what's going on? _____
_____
_____
_____
_____
_____
_____
_____
_____
_____
_____

ok. describe how you're feeling: _____
_____
_____
_____
_____
_____
_____
_____
_____

now, what are you thinking? _____
_____
_____
_____
_____
_____

what evidence supports that thought?   what about evidence that contradicts it?

_____   _____
_____   _____
_____   _____
_____   _____
_____   _____
_____   _____
_____   _____
_____   _____
_____   _____
_____   _____
_____   _____

got it. let's try writing down an alternative thought: _____

_____
_____
_____
_____
_____

how do you feel now? _____

_____
_____

anything else before you go? _____

_____
_____
_____

IV

date _____   day (circle one)   sun   mon   tue   wed   thu   fri   sa

time _____   where are you right now? _____

so, what's going on? _____

_____

_____

_____

_____

_____

_____

_____

_____

_____

_____

ok. describe how you're feeling: _____

_____

_____

_____

_____

_____

_____

_____

now, what are you thinking? _____

_____

_____

_____

_____

what evidence supports that thought?

what about evidence that contradicts it?

_____   _____
_____   _____
_____   _____
_____   _____
_____   _____
_____   _____
_____   _____
_____   _____
_____   _____
_____   _____
_____   _____

got it. let's try writing down an alternative thought: _____

_____
_____
_____
_____
_____

how do you feel now? _____

_____
_____
_____

anything else before you go? _____

_____
_____
_____
_____

use this page to reflect on the progress you've made.
have you idenfitied recurring triggers and anxious feelings?
are you starting to think in a more constructive way?

tell me about it.

date _____   day (circle one)   sun   mon   tue   wed   thu   fri   sat

time _____   where are you right now? _____

so, what's going on? _____
_____
_____
_____
_____
_____
_____
_____
_____
_____

ok. describe how you're feeling: _____
_____
_____
_____
_____
_____
_____
_____
_____

now, what are you thinking? _____
_____
_____
_____
_____
_____

what evidence supports that thought?

what about evidence that contradicts it?

_____

_____

got it. let's try writing down an alternative thought: _____

_____

ow do you feel now? _____

_____

nything else before you go? _____

_____

IV

date _____   day (circle one)   sun   mon   tue   wed   thu   fri   sat

time _____   where are you right now? _____

so, what's going on? _____

_____

_____

_____

_____

_____

_____

_____

_____

_____

ok. describe how you're feeling: _____

_____

_____

_____

_____

_____

_____

_____

now, what are you thinking? _____

_____

_____

_____

_____

what evidence supports that thought?

what about evidence that contradicts it?

_____   _____
_____   _____
_____   _____
_____   _____
_____   _____
_____   _____
_____   _____
_____   _____
_____   _____
_____   _____
_____   _____

got it. let's try writing down an alternative thought: _____

_____
_____
_____
_____
_____
_____

how do you feel now? _____

_____
_____

anything else before you go? _____

_____
_____
_____
_____

date _____ day (circle one)   sun   mon   tue   wed   thu   fri   sat

time _____ where are you right now? _____

so, what's going on? _____

_____

_____

_____

_____

_____

_____

_____

_____

_____

ok. describe how you're feeling: _____

_____

_____

_____

_____

_____

_____

_____

now, what are you thinking? _____

_____

_____

_____

_____

what evidence supports that thought?

what about evidence that contradicts it?

_____
_____
_____
_____
_____
_____
_____
_____
_____
_____
_____
_____

got it. let's try writing down an alternative thought: _____

_____
_____
_____
_____
_____

how do you feel now? _____

_____
_____

anything else before you go? _____

_____
_____
_____

date _____ day (circle one)　　sun　　mon　　tue　　wed　　thu　　fri　　sat

time _____ where are you right now? _____

so, what's going on? _____

_____

_____

_____

_____

_____

_____

_____

_____

_____

ok. describe how you're feeling: _____

_____

_____

_____

_____

_____

_____

_____

now, what are you thinking? _____

_____

_____

_____

_____

what evidence supports that thought?

_____
_____
_____
_____
_____
_____
_____
_____
_____
_____
_____

what about evidence that contradicts it

_____
_____
_____
_____
_____
_____
_____
_____
_____
_____
_____

got it. let's try writing down an alternative thought: _____

_____
_____
_____
_____
_____

how do you feel now? _____

_____
_____

anything else before you go? _____

_____
_____
_____
_____

date _____   day (circle one)   sun   mon   tue   wed   thu   fri   sat

time _____   where are you right now? _____

so, what's going on? _____

_____

_____

_____

_____

_____

_____

_____

_____

_____

ok. describe how you're feeling: _____

_____

_____

_____

_____

_____

_____

_____

_____

now, what are you thinking? _____

_____

_____

_____

_____

_____

what evidence supports that thought?

_____
_____
_____
_____
_____
_____
_____
_____
_____
_____
_____
_____

what about evidence that contradicts it?

_____
_____
_____
_____
_____
_____
_____
_____
_____
_____
_____
_____

got it. let's try writing down an alternative thought: _____

_____
_____
_____
_____
_____

how do you feel now? _____

_____
_____
_____

anything else before you go? _____

_____
_____
_____
_____

date _____   day (circle one)   sun   mon   tue   wed   thu   fri   sa

time _____   where are you right now? _____

so, what's going on? _____

_____

_____

_____

_____

_____

_____

_____

_____

_____

ok. describe how you're feeling: _____

_____

_____

_____

_____

_____

_____

_____

_____

now, what are you thinking? _____

_____

_____

_____

_____

_____

what evidence supports that thought?

what about evidence that contradicts it?

_____

_____

_____

_____

_____

_____

_____

_____

_____

_____

_____

got it. let's try writing down an alternative thought: _____

_____

_____

_____

_____

how do you feel now? _____

_____

_____

anything else before you go? _____

_____

_____

_____

date _____   day (circle one)   sun   mon   tue   wed   thu   fri   sat

time _____   where are you right now? _____

so, what's going on? _____

_____

_____

_____

_____

_____

_____

_____

_____

_____

ok. describe how you're feeling: _____

_____

_____

_____

_____

_____

_____

_____

_____

now, what are you thinking? _____

_____

_____

_____

_____

what evidence supports that thought?   what about evidence that contradicts it?

_____   _____
_____   _____
_____   _____
_____   _____
_____   _____
_____   _____
_____   _____
_____   _____
_____   _____
_____   _____
_____   _____

got it. let's try writing down an alternative thought: _____

_____
_____
_____
_____
_____

how do you feel now? _____

_____
_____
_____

anything else before you go? _____

_____
_____
_____
_____

date _____   day (circle one)   sun   mon   tue   wed   thu   fri   sat

time _____   where are you right now? _____

so, what's going on? _____
_____
_____
_____
_____
_____
_____
_____
_____
_____
_____

ok. describe how you're feeling: _____
_____
_____
_____
_____
_____
_____
_____
_____

now, what are you thinking? _____
_____
_____
_____
_____

what evidence supports that thought?

what about evidence that contradicts it?

_____

_____

got it. let's try writing down an alternative thought: _____

_____

how do you feel now? _____

_____

anything else before you go? _____

_____

IV

date _____   day (circle one)   sun   mon   tue   wed   thu   fri   sa

time _____   where are you right now? _____

so, what's going on? _____

_____

_____

_____

_____

_____

_____

_____

_____

_____

_____

ok. describe how you're feeling: _____

_____

_____

_____

_____

_____

_____

_____

_____

_____

now, what are you thinking? _____

_____

_____

_____

_____

_____

what evidence supports that thought?

what about evidence that contradicts it?

_____

_____

_____

_____

_____

_____

_____

_____

_____

_____

_____

_____

got it. let's try writing down an alternative thought: _____

_____

_____

_____

_____

_____

how do you feel now? _____

_____

_____

_____

anything else before you go? _____

_____

_____

_____

use this page to reflect on the progress you've made.
have you idenfitied recurring triggers and anxious feelings?
are you starting to think in a more constructive way?

tell me about it.

date _____ day (circle one)   sun   mon   tue   wed   thu   fri   sat

time _____ where are you right now? _____

so, what's going on? _____

_____

_____

_____

_____

_____

_____

_____

_____

_____

ok. describe how you're feeling: _____

_____

_____

_____

_____

_____

_____

_____

now, what are you thinking? _____

_____

_____

_____

_____

what evidence supports that thought?

what about evidence that contradicts it?

got it. let's try writing down an alternative thought: _____

how do you feel now? _____

anything else before you go? _____

date _____   day (circle one)   sun   mon   tue   wed   thu   fri   sat

time _____   where are you right now? _____

so, what's going on? _____

_____

_____

_____

_____

_____

_____

_____

_____

_____

ok. describe how you're feeling: _____

_____

_____

_____

_____

_____

_____

_____

now, what are you thinking? _____

_____

_____

_____

_____

what evidence supports that thought?

what about evidence that contradicts it?

got it. let's try writing down an alternative thought: _____

how do you feel now? _____

anything else before you go? _____

date _____   day (circle one)   sun   mon   tue   wed   thu   fri   sat

time _____   where are you right now? _____

so, what's going on? _____

_____

_____

_____

_____

_____

_____

_____

_____

_____

ok. describe how you're feeling: _____

_____

_____

_____

_____

_____

_____

_____

now, what are you thinking? _____

_____

_____

_____

_____

what evidence supports that thought?

_____
_____
_____
_____
_____
_____
_____
_____
_____
_____
_____
_____

what about evidence that contradicts it?

_____
_____
_____
_____
_____
_____
_____
_____
_____
_____
_____
_____

got it. let's try writing down an alternative thought: _____

_____
_____
_____
_____
_____
_____

how do you feel now? _____

_____
_____

anything else before you go? _____

_____
_____
_____

date _____ day (circle one)　　sun　　mon　　tue　　wed　　thu　　fri　　sa

time _____ where are you right now? _____

so, what's going on? _____
_____
_____
_____
_____
_____
_____
_____
_____
_____

ok. describe how you're feeling: _____
_____
_____
_____
_____
_____
_____
_____
_____

now, what are you thinking? _____
_____
_____
_____
_____

what evidence supports that thought?

what about evidence that contradicts it?

got it. let's try writing down an alternative thought: _____

ow do you feel now? _____

anything else before you go? _____

date _____   day (circle one)   sun   mon   tue   wed   thu   fri   sat

time _____   where are you right now? _____

so, what's going on? _____
_____
_____
_____
_____
_____
_____
_____
_____
_____

ok. describe how you're feeling: _____
_____
_____
_____
_____
_____
_____
_____
_____

now, what are you thinking? _____
_____
_____
_____
_____
_____

what evidence supports that thought?   what about evidence that contradicts it?

_____   _____
_____   _____
_____   _____
_____   _____
_____   _____
_____   _____
_____   _____
_____   _____
_____   _____
_____   _____
_____   _____

got it. let's try writing down an alternative thought: _____

_____
_____
_____
_____
_____

how do you feel now? _____

_____
_____

anything else before you go? _____

_____
_____
_____

date _____   day (circle one)   sun   mon   tue   wed   thu   fri   sat

time _____   where are you right now? _____

so, what's going on? _____

_____

_____

_____

_____

_____

_____

_____

_____

_____

ok. describe how you're feeling: _____

_____

_____

_____

_____

_____

_____

_____

now, what are you thinking? _____

_____

_____

_____

_____

what evidence supports that thought?   what about evidence that contradicts it?

_____   _____

_____   _____

_____   _____

_____   _____

_____   _____

_____   _____

_____   _____

_____   _____

_____   _____

_____   _____

got it. let's try writing down an alternative thought: _____

_____

_____

_____

_____

_____

how do you feel now? _____

_____

_____

_____

anything else before you go? _____

_____

_____

_____

_____

IV

date _____   day (circle one)   sun   mon   tue   wed   thu   fri   sat

time _____   where are you right now? _____

so, what's going on? _____
_____
_____
_____
_____
_____
_____
_____
_____
_____
_____

ok. describe how you're feeling: _____
_____
_____
_____
_____
_____
_____
_____
_____

now, what are you thinking? _____
_____
_____
_____
_____

what evidence supports that thought?

what about evidence that contradicts it?

_____
_____
_____
_____
_____
_____
_____
_____
_____
_____
_____

got it. let's try writing down an alternative thought: _____

_____
_____
_____
_____
_____

how do you feel now? _____

_____
_____
_____

anything else before you go? _____

_____
_____
_____
_____

date _____   day (circle one)   sun   mon   tue   wed   thu   fri   sat

time _____   where are you right now? _____

so, what's going on? _____

_____

_____

_____

_____

_____

_____

_____

_____

_____

_____

ok. describe how you're feeling: _____

_____

_____

_____

_____

_____

_____

_____

_____

now, what are you thinking? _____

_____

_____

_____

_____

_____

what evidence supports that thought?

_____
_____
_____
_____
_____
_____
_____
_____
_____
_____
_____
_____

what about evidence that contradicts it?

_____
_____
_____
_____
_____
_____
_____
_____
_____
_____
_____
_____

got it. let's try writing down an alternative thought: _____

_____
_____
_____
_____
_____
_____

how do you feel now? _____

_____
_____
_____

anything else before you go? _____

_____
_____
_____
_____

date _____ day (circle one) sun mon tue wed thu fri sat

time _____ where are you right now? _____

so, what's going on? _____

_____

_____

_____

_____

_____

_____

_____

_____

_____

ok. describe how you're feeling: _____

_____

_____

_____

_____

_____

_____

_____

_____

now, what are you thinking? _____

_____

_____

_____

_____

_____

what evidence supports that thought?

_____
_____
_____
_____
_____
_____
_____
_____
_____
_____
_____
_____

what about evidence that contradicts it?

_____
_____
_____
_____
_____
_____
_____
_____
_____
_____
_____
_____

got it. let's try writing down an alternative thought: _____

_____
_____
_____
_____
_____
_____

how do you feel now? _____

_____
_____
_____

anything else before you go? _____

_____
_____
_____
_____

use this page to reflect on the progress you've made.
have you idenfitied recurring triggers and anxious feelings?
are you starting to think in a more constructive way?

tell me about it.

_____

_____

_____

_____

_____

_____

_____

_____

_____

_____

_____

_____

_____

_____

_____

_____

_____

_____

_____

_____

_____

_____

_____

_____

_____

_____

_____

date _____   day (circle one)   sun   mon   tue   wed   thu   fri   sat

time _____   where are you right now? _____

so, what's going on? _____

_____

_____

_____

_____

_____

_____

_____

_____

_____

ok. describe how you're feeling: _____

_____

_____

_____

_____

_____

_____

_____

now, what are you thinking? _____

_____

_____

_____

_____

_____

what evidence supports that thought?

what about evidence that contradicts it?

got it. let's try writing down an alternative thought: _____

how do you feel now? _____

anything else before you go? _____

date _____ day (circle one)   sun   mon   tue   wed   thu   fri   sat

time _____ where are you right now? _____

so, what's going on? _____

_____

_____

_____

_____

_____

_____

_____

_____

_____

ok. describe how you're feeling: _____

_____

_____

_____

_____

_____

_____

_____

now, what are you thinking? _____

_____

_____

_____

_____

_____

what evidence supports that thought?

what about evidence that contradicts it?

_____   _____
_____   _____
_____   _____
_____   _____
_____   _____
_____   _____
_____   _____
_____   _____
_____   _____
_____   _____
_____   _____
_____   _____

got it. let's try writing down an alternative thought: _____

_____
_____
_____
_____
_____

how do you feel now? _____

_____
_____

anything else before you go? _____

_____
_____
_____

date _____ day (circle one)   sun   mon   tue   wed   thu   fri   sat

time _____ where are you right now? _____

so, what's going on? _____
_____
_____
_____
_____
_____
_____
_____
_____
_____
_____

ok. describe how you're feeling: _____
_____
_____
_____
_____
_____
_____
_____
_____

now, what are you thinking? _____
_____
_____
_____
_____

what evidence supports that thought?   what about evidence that contradicts it?

_____   _____
_____   _____
_____   _____
_____   _____
_____   _____
_____   _____
_____   _____
_____   _____
_____   _____
_____   _____
_____   _____

got it. let's try writing down an alternative thought: _____

_____
_____
_____
_____
_____

how do you feel now? _____

_____
_____
_____

anything else before you go? _____

_____
_____
_____
_____

date _____   day (circle one)   sun   mon   tue   wed   thu   fri   sat

time _____   where are you right now? _____

so, what's going on? _____

_____

_____

_____

_____

_____

_____

_____

_____

_____

ok. describe how you're feeling: _____

_____

_____

_____

_____

_____

_____

_____

now, what are you thinking? _____

_____

_____

_____

_____

what evidence supports that thought?

what about evidence that contradicts it?

_____

got it. let's try writing down an alternative thought: _____

how do you feel now? _____

anything else before you go? _____

date _____   day (circle one)   sun   mon   tue   wed   thu   fri   sat

time _____   where are you right now? _____

so, what's going on? _____

_____

_____

_____

_____

_____

_____

_____

_____

_____

ok. describe how you're feeling: _____

_____

_____

_____

_____

_____

_____

_____

now, what are you thinking? _____

_____

_____

_____

_____

what evidence supports that thought?

_____
_____
_____
_____
_____
_____
_____
_____
_____
_____
_____
_____

what about evidence that contradicts it?

_____
_____
_____
_____
_____
_____
_____
_____
_____
_____
_____
_____

got it. let's try writing down an alternative thought: _____

_____
_____
_____
_____
_____
_____

how do you feel now? _____

_____
_____
_____

anything else before you go? _____

_____
_____
_____
_____

date _____   day (circle one)   sun   mon   tue   wed   thu   fri   sat

time _____   where are you right now? _____

so, what's going on? _____

_____

_____

_____

_____

_____

_____

_____

_____

_____

ok. describe how you're feeling: _____

_____

_____

_____

_____

_____

_____

_____

now, what are you thinking? _____

_____

_____

_____

_____

_____

what evidence supports that thought?

_____
_____
_____
_____
_____
_____
_____
_____
_____
_____
_____
_____

what about evidence that contradicts it?

_____
_____
_____
_____
_____
_____
_____
_____
_____
_____
_____
_____

got it. let's try writing down an alternative thought: _____

_____
_____
_____
_____
_____

how do you feel now? _____

_____
_____
_____

anything else before you go? _____

_____
_____
_____
_____

date _____ day (circle one)   sun   mon   tue   wed   thu   fri   sat

time _____ where are you right now? _____

so, what's going on? _____

_____

_____

_____

_____

_____

_____

_____

_____

_____

ok. describe how you're feeling: _____

_____

_____

_____

_____

_____

_____

_____

now, what are you thinking? _____

_____

_____

_____

_____

what evidence supports that thought?

_____

what about evidence that contradicts it?

got it. let's try writing down an alternative thought: _____

how do you feel now? _____

anything else before you go? _____

date _____ day (circle one) sun mon tue wed thu fri sat

time _____ where are you right now? _____

so, what's going on? _____
_____
_____
_____
_____
_____
_____
_____
_____
_____

ok. describe how you're feeling: _____
_____
_____
_____
_____
_____
_____
_____

now, what are you thinking? _____
_____
_____
_____
_____
_____

what evidence supports that thought?

_____
_____
_____
_____
_____
_____
_____
_____
_____
_____
_____

what about evidence that contradicts it?

_____
_____
_____
_____
_____
_____
_____
_____
_____
_____
_____

got it. let's try writing down an alternative thought: _____
_____
_____
_____
_____
_____

how do you feel now? _____
_____
_____

anything else before you go? _____
_____
_____
_____

date _____   day (circle one)   sun   mon   tue   wed   thu   fri   sat

time _____   where are you right now? _____

so, what's going on? _____
_____
_____
_____
_____
_____
_____
_____
_____
_____
_____

ok. describe how you're feeling: _____
_____
_____
_____
_____
_____
_____
_____
_____

now, what are you thinking? _____
_____
_____
_____
_____
_____

what evidence supports that thought?

what about evidence that contradicts it?

got it. let's try writing down an alternative thought: _____

how do you feel now? _____

anything else before you go? _____

use this page to reflect on the progress you've made.
have you idenfitied recurring triggers and anxious feelings?
are you starting to think in a more constructive way?

tell me about it.

date _____   day (circle one)   sun   mon   tue   wed   thu   fri   sat

time _____   where are you right now? _____

so, what's going on? _____

_____

_____

_____

_____

_____

_____

_____

_____

ok. describe how you're feeling: _____

_____

_____

_____

_____

_____

_____

now, what are you thinking? _____

_____

_____

_____

_____

what evidence supports that thought?

_____
_____
_____
_____
_____
_____
_____
_____
_____
_____
_____

what about evidence that contradicts it?

_____
_____
_____
_____
_____
_____
_____
_____
_____
_____
_____

got it. let's try writing down an alternative thought: _____

_____
_____
_____
_____
_____

how do you feel now? _____

_____
_____

anything else before you go? _____

_____
_____
_____

date _____   day (circle one)   sun   mon   tue   wed   thu   fri   sat

time _____   where are you right now? _____

so, what's going on? _____

_____

_____

_____

_____

_____

_____

_____

_____

_____

ok. describe how you're feeling: _____

_____

_____

_____

_____

_____

_____

_____

now, what are you thinking? _____

_____

_____

_____

_____

_____

what evidence supports that thought?

_____
_____
_____
_____
_____
_____
_____
_____
_____
_____
_____
_____

what about evidence that contradicts it?

_____
_____
_____
_____
_____
_____
_____
_____
_____
_____
_____
_____

got it. let's try writing down an alternative thought: _____

_____
_____
_____
_____
_____

how do you feel now? _____

_____
_____

anything else before you go? _____

_____
_____
_____

date _____ day (circle one)   sun   mon   tue   wed   thu   fri   sat

time _____ where are you right now? _____

so, what's going on? _____

_____

_____

_____

_____

_____

_____

_____

_____

_____

ok. describe how you're feeling: _____

_____

_____

_____

_____

_____

_____

_____

_____

now, what are you thinking? _____

_____

_____

_____

_____

_____

what evidence supports that thought?　　　　what about evidence that contradicts it?

_____　　_____
_____　　_____
_____　　_____
_____　　_____
_____　　_____
_____　　_____
_____　　_____
_____　　_____
_____　　_____
_____　　_____
_____　　_____

got it. let's try writing down an alternative thought: _____

_____
_____
_____
_____
_____

how do you feel now? _____

_____
_____
_____

anything else before you go? _____

_____
_____
_____
_____

date _____   day (circle one)   sun   mon   tue   wed   thu   fri   sat

time _____   where are you right now? _____

so, what's going on? _____

_____

_____

_____

_____

_____

_____

_____

_____

_____

ok. describe how you're feeling: _____

_____

_____

_____

_____

_____

_____

_____

now, what are you thinking? _____

_____

_____

_____

_____

_____

what evidence supports that thought?

_____

_____

what about evidence that contradicts it?

_____

got it. let's try writing down an alternative thought: _____

how do you feel now? _____

anything else before you go? _____

date _____   day (circle one)   sun   mon   tue   wed   thu   fri   sat

time _____   where are you right now? _____

so, what's going on? _____

_____

_____

_____

_____

_____

_____

_____

_____

_____

ok. describe how you're feeling: _____

_____

_____

_____

_____

_____

_____

_____

now, what are you thinking? _____

_____

_____

_____

_____

IV

what evidence supports that thought?

_____
_____
_____
_____
_____
_____
_____
_____
_____
_____
_____
_____

what about evidence that contradicts it?

_____
_____
_____
_____
_____
_____
_____
_____
_____
_____
_____

got it. let's try writing down an alternative thought: _____

_____
_____
_____
_____
_____

how do you feel now? _____

_____
_____
_____

anything else before you go? _____

_____
_____
_____
_____

IV

date _____   day (circle one)   sun   mon   tue   wed   thu   fri   sat

time _____   where are you right now? _____

so, what's going on? _____

_____

_____

_____

_____

_____

_____

_____

_____

_____

_____

ok. describe how you're feeling: _____

_____

_____

_____

_____

_____

_____

_____

_____

now, what are you thinking? _____

_____

_____

_____

_____

what evidence supports that thought?

_____

_____

_____

_____

_____

_____

_____

_____

_____

_____

_____

_____

what about evidence that contradicts it?

_____

_____

_____

_____

_____

_____

_____

_____

_____

_____

_____

got it. let's try writing down an alternative thought: _____

_____

_____

_____

_____

_____

how do you feel now? _____

_____

_____

anything else before you go? _____

_____

_____

_____

date _____   day (circle one)   sun   mon   tue   wed   thu   fri   sat

time _____   where are you right now? _____

so, what's going on? _____

_____

_____

_____

_____

_____

_____

_____

_____

_____

_____

ok. describe how you're feeling: _____

_____

_____

_____

_____

_____

_____

_____

_____

now, what are you thinking? _____

_____

_____

_____

_____

_____

what evidence supports that thought?

_____
_____
_____
_____
_____
_____
_____
_____
_____
_____
_____
_____

what about evidence that contradicts it?

_____
_____
_____
_____
_____
_____
_____
_____
_____
_____
_____

got it. let's try writing down an alternative thought: _____

_____
_____
_____
_____
_____
_____

how do you feel now? _____

_____
_____
_____

anything else before you go? _____

_____
_____
_____
_____

date _____   day (circle one)   sun   mon   tue   wed   thu   fri   sat

time _____   where are you right now? _____

so, what's going on? _____

_____

_____

_____

_____

_____

_____

_____

_____

_____

ok. describe how you're feeling: _____

_____

_____

_____

_____

_____

_____

_____

now, what are you thinking? _____

_____

_____

_____

_____

what evidence supports that thought?

_____
_____
_____
_____
_____
_____
_____
_____
_____
_____
_____
_____

what about evidence that contradicts it?

_____
_____
_____
_____
_____
_____
_____
_____
_____
_____
_____

got it. let's try writing down an alternative thought. _____

_____
_____
_____
_____
_____
_____

how do you feel now? _____

_____
_____
_____

anything else before you go? _____

_____
_____
_____
_____

IV

use this page to reflect on the progress you've made.
have you idenfitied recurring triggers and anxious feelings?
are you starting to think in a more constructive way?

tell me about it.

_____
_____
_____
_____
_____
_____
_____
_____
_____
_____
_____
_____
_____
_____
_____
_____
_____
_____
_____
_____
_____
_____
_____
_____
_____
_____
_____
_____
_____
_____
_____
_____
_____

IV